SEASONS

OF THE

HEART

S EASONS

OF THE

H EART

Perennial Wisdom

on Moving Through the

Cycles of Our Relationships

THE HAZELDEN FOUNDATION

A Hazelden Book
HarperCollins*Publishers*

FIRST HARPERCOLLINS EDITION PUBLISHED IN 1993.

Library of Congress Cataloging-in-Publication Data

Seasons of the heart : perennial wisdom on moving through the cycles
    of our relationships / the Hazelden Foundation. — 1st Harper Collins ed.
        p. cm.
      "A Hazelden book."
      Includes indexes.
      ISBN 0-06-255290-2 (alk. paper)
      1. Interpersonal relations—Quotations, maxims, etc.   I. Hazelden
    Foundation.
    PN6084.I5S43   1993
    081–dc20   92–56398
                                                                  CIP

93 94 95 96 97 ❖ HAD 10 9 8 7 6 5 4 3 2 1

This edition is printed on acid-free paper that meets the American National
Standards Institute Z39.48 Standard.

$\int$ ometimes as
the cycles or seasons of
relationships change, the
boundaries and dimensions
of relationships change.

We can learn to
be flexible enough to go
through and accept these
changing seasons.

Melody Beattie

C O N T E N T S

PREFACE

Many of us say that our greatest blessings are the people in our lives. Whether we are talking about spouses, significant others, children, parents, friends, or co-workers, these personal connections are what we most value in our daily comings and goings.

This book is a collection of quotes from more than forty of Hazelden's most inspiring authors. Through the years, these authors have explored many ways of sustaining meaningful relationships with others. Sometimes that means facing our fears and taking risks. Sometimes it means being patient and letting others learn their own lessons. At other times, relating well to others requires us to lighten up and be open to the joy that surrounds us. At still other times, our relationships call us to grieve, let go, and say good-bye.

Relationships, then, seem to take on a natural evolution as we grow and change. To reflect this process, the quotes here have been arranged into four themes: "Beginnings," "Nurturing What We Have," "Enjoying Life," and "Letting Go."

The quotes included here are ultimately intended to affirm the natural ebb and flow of our various relationships and help us more fully appreciate the many people in our life—regardless of how new or established the bonds with these people may be.

BEGINNINGS

*N*ew beginnings are exciting. They awaken us with fresh feelings, thoughts, and experiences. If we bring everything we have learned to them, they can be better than anything we've experienced in the past. Each new beginning is a chance to discover more about ourselves and others, to stretch ourselves in new ways, to learn how much we have to give and how much others can give to us.

Veronica Ray

It doesn't matter what the results are, just as long as we act. Each of us is interesting, thrilling, and exciting. In fact, we're probably attracted to qualities we see in other people that we haven't yet recognized in ourselves.

Perry Tilleraas

*T*hose people close to us and those just passing through our lives have reason to be there. Giving attention to another's humanity is our calling.

Karen Casey

Giving away our power to the whims of others weakens our Spirit. Personal freedom means choosing our own behavior; it means acting rather than reacting.

Karen Casey

Each day is a new creation, and each day brings new lessons and opportunities. We build on what is past, but we do not need to repeat it.

Elizabeth L.

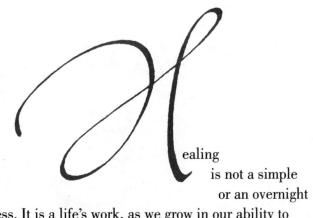ealing
is not a simple
or an overnight
process. It is a life's work, as we grow in our ability to
allow love into our injured hearts.

Ruth Schweitzer-Mordecai

Healthy connections to another start with self-love, for it is up to me to embrace and nurture myself. In this way I can always be whole.

Will Limon

I feel the stirrings of something profound, something central to my life, all life. I sense the beginnings of love. Like the smallest green tendril winding toward the sun, my love grows. It is love for myself and for the opportunity of life. I know this love will blossom someday into the willingness to be vulnerable again.

Will Limon

*I*f we are truly loved and capable of functioning in loving relationships, what else really matters? What else is there? We may never have all the things we once thought were justly owed us, we may never be as able to play as we think we should, we may never know all we think we should know. But if we are able to glory in and share in the love around us, then we shall have found the key which makes life worth living.

Earnie Larsen and Carol Larsen Hegarty

The special meaning of birthdays can become a reminder that we are called on to be reborn regularly. Seeing new beauty is a kind of rebirth. Making a decision, no matter how small, that enhances our life is a form of rebirth. Moving on to a new place, a new state of freedom, is being born again. Every day can be a birthday.

Earnie Larsen and Carol Larsen Hegarty

I have learned to view all circumstances in my life as lessons for my growth process. Trusting my intuition—that calm, inner voice that we each possess—has helped me realize how the principle of *synchronicity* works in all our lives. Synchronicity is that powerful sense of spiritual coincidence—that chance meeting, that lucky break.

Helene Lerner-Robbins

How many times do we say no instead of yes? We let countless opportunities go by because we lack the imagination to visualize their possibilities.

Helene Lerner-Robbins

The baby takes a step, totters, and falls, only to pull himself up and begin again. Eventually, he learns to walk, not because each step was a success but because he is always ready to *try again.*

You can reach your goals in exactly the same way— by taking as many baby steps as you need to and always allowing yourself to try again.

Marie Lindquist

*S*omeday we may find a new lover and new friends, but until then, our solitude doesn't have to be unhappy. We can love ourselves regardless of other relationships in our lives.

Veronica Ray

*A*lthough the day is done, tomorrow is yet to come. There are plans to make, places to go, people to see, and projects to do. Tomorrow can begin with hope and strength and energy directed to all our forthcoming events.

Amy E. Dean

Succeeding alone means we have survived; succeeding with others means we have truly lived. We were not put into this life to survive without others, but to live with them. By joining ourselves with the humanity around us, we have joined that spirit which connects us all.

Amy E. Dean

I have learned that the power of love to transform our lives is actually in all of our relationships. It's often not ecstatic, and there are far more than three or four kinds of relationships. Some are deep, intimate, lifetime partnership commitments, such as a marriage. Some are caring friendships. Some are casual acquaintances with people we see occasionally in our neighborhood, at our children's school, or at work. All of these kinds of relationships carry the power of love that transforms and heals.

Merle Fossum

It is often said that to love someone, we must first love ourselves. Yet, I believe it is equally true that the more we feel love for and from other people, the more we learn to love ourselves.

Merle Fossum

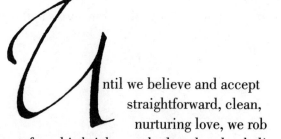ntil we believe and accept straightforward, clean, nurturing love, we rob ourselves of our birthright—to be loved and to believe that we are lovable.

Jean Illsley Clarke and Connie Dawson

When we give in to love, when we remove the barriers to love and surrender to it, we are back home where we're supposed to be. We are who we're supposed to be.

Mark L.

Our goal is to find our way back to the human community. We need to convert the longing to be accepted and loved into positive action. We may have to remind ourselves many times that we have the inherent right to be human.

Ronald Potter-Efron and Patricia Potter-Efron

A relationship doesn't begin our life; a relationship doesn't become our life. A relationship is a continuation of life. While a special love relationship may meet certain needs that only a special love relationship can meet, it won't meet all our needs and it won't "make us happy."

Melody Beattie

Learning to feel lovable—capable and worthy of being loved—is the most powerful feeling of all. It opens the door for us to connect with other people; it keeps out shame; it inspires us to recreate our life according to our dreams. As our lovableness quotient increases, so do our feelings of self-esteem. If we are not in charge of our self-esteem, someone else will be. And that is not what we want.

Kristin A. Kunzman

You are right to be cautious and a little apprehensive in new situations. Let yourself feel the fear of change. Let the threat of the new come to the surface, and then it can pass. Denying the threat of the new will keep you in the old.

Judi Hollis

If you take the attitude that everything that is happening is important, you will be able to find the silver lining in the events of your life.

Sheila Bayle-Lissick and Elise Marquam Jahns

Relationships are a matrix within which we either grow or wither. Nowhere but in a relationship do we encounter ourselves so directly and so clearly at our best and our worst.

Brenda Schaeffer

My belief is that love calls us to a state of wakefulness where we experience a freshness of spirit and freedom from a polluted mind. This calls for a grounding in our own goodness. If we want love, if we want to help the world, we have to take this personal journey. It is up to each of us to experience our own meaning and take that meaning into all of our relationships.

Brenda Schaeffer

I had shouted at God, "Show me you love me," looking for a thunderbolt as proof.

Instead, God had whispered, "Look around you."

Heidi Waldrop

*W*hatever lies before me
is not blocking my next step;
it *is* my next step.

Maureen Brady

When I admit my powerlessness over things not within my control, I free my energy to change those things I can change.

Maureen Brady

Acceptance is always the first step in healing, as paradoxical as that may seem. We need to work with ourselves and with others from where we actually are now, not from where we would like to be.

Molly Young Brown

So far, I have never failed to detect God's will for me at any moment if I sought it, listened for it, and really welcomed it.

Eliot Alexander

Nurturing
WHAT WE HAVE

Wanting to control other people, to make them live as we'd have them live, makes the attainment of serenity impossible.

Karen Casey

*T*here are times when we simply *must* speak up firmly for our rights. If *we* don't speak up, nobody will. We have to let people know what's on our minds. We don't transmit thoughts on a special "spouse wavelength," and our spouse doesn't have a built-in receiver that picks up random ruminations of discontent.

Gayle Rosellini and Mark Worden

One of the most important things we can do to calm another person is *help them save face.* Nobody wants to end up looking like a fool, and a person will often cling stubbornly to an idea they know is stupid rather than admit their mistake.

Gayle Rosellini and Mark Worden

We need to find a balance between solving problems and learning to live with unsolved problems. Much of our anguish comes from having to live with the grief of unsolved problems and having things not go the way we hoped and expected.

Melody Beattie

Forgiveness gives us personal power that we never had when we tried to have power over others. It frees us to do the work we were meant to do. And sometimes, it gives us a way to love someone without pain.

Stephanie Abbott

The ideal relationship is one in which each partner strives to grow. It is an ever-expanding commitment, mutually supportive of each person's need for change and growth.

Liane Cordes

By expressing our thoughts and feelings out loud to another person, we become better able to understand and deal with whatever is bothering us. More important, we deepen our relationships with family and friends when we are willing to communicate on a meaningful level.

Elizabeth L.

Although I am responsible for my thoughts about myself, I am affected by those around me. I need to evaluate the benefits of a relationship in which it is difficult to feel okay about myself.

Ruth Schweitzer-Mordecai

Today we need not think about whether our wishes will materialize. We can simply take action and let go of the results. In this way, we wear the world like a loose garment, without trying to manipulate situations so they go our way.

Helene Lerner-Robbins

There is simply no good reason for resisting chances to enjoy the relaxation that comes when I am not in charge. Relying on others really is a pretty good feeling.

Eliot Alexander

It's important that you learn to play both roles—the giver and the receiver. If you only know how to make disclosures but don't know how to receive them, you will thwart the ritual of sharing necessary for true intimacy.

Marie Lindquist

As we grow, we learn how to move freely and at the same time avoid stepping on each other's toes (most of the time). As we become more graceful, we can express our own feelings without injuring the other person.

Elizabeth L.

Our most effective use of each day means believing we can accomplish something. There is time to be grateful for each day's experiences. There is time to build relationships with ourselves and others. Each day there is time to grow.

Amy E. Dean

Interdependence is the art of loving without being consumed. It is the art of caring for another without denying ourselves. It implies attending to another's needs while keeping our own needs in view. Other words for interdependence include feeling connected, in touch, engaged, or caring. As such, interdependence means gaining a sense of joy and serenity that *includes* the person we care for but not *depending* on that person.

Mel Pohl, Deniston Kay, and Doug Toft

The art of nurturing adults consists of an elegant balance—being sensitive about when to offer assertive care and when to offer support. Not too little, not too much.

Jean Illsley Clarke and Connie Dawson

Openness to change can be risky—it can even lead to breakups—but without it, a relationship will lose its vibrancy.

Brenda Schaeffer

Reliability doesn't mean that people won't get angry or misunderstand or that they won't ever hurt each other. It means they will be accountable for their actions. And it means they can see what is coming in one another's reactions and can feel some influence over each other. Our relationship with a friend is affirmed when we can count on certain things to make them angry, to make them laugh, or to touch their love.

Merle Fossum

Apology is difficult, but it doesn't require your humiliation or self-denigration. Shame only distracts you from the repair you have set out to do. Making amends acknowledges the truth and takes responsibility for the consequences without the sackcloth and ashes.

Roseann Lloyd and Merle Fossum

We got help by helping others. We gained love by sharing love. We were released from judgment when we quit judging. We know the help, the love, and the release are not permanent; our possession of them is based on our willingness, hour by hour, to give them away.

Mark L.

Good shame . . . is a temporary state that tells us something is seriously wrong in our relationship with the world. It tells us that the connection between us and other people is broken and needs fixing. Good shame is like having a true friend, one who is not afraid to tell you that you are messing up your life. A good friend may sometimes have to tell you the truth, even when that truth is painful to both of you.

Ronald Potter-Efron and Patricia Potter-Efron

Trust is the basis of any relationship, whether the relationship is within oneself or with others. If a relationship is not based on trust, the relationship becomes a struggle. The same is true for the relationship we have with ourselves. Trust allows us the ability to heal and the freedom to connect with others.

Craig Nakken

A major way we support another person in a relationship is by keeping the person safe from our own nastiness. . . . We may feel like getting mean, but in a healthy relationship we choose the relationship over any momentary sense of power we might think we get from being mean to the other person.

Craig Nakken

*T*rue intimacy is feeling connected to another person in times of quiet and peace as well as in times of stress. It is being able to *trust* that another person cares about you and that you care about him or her. It is something that grows stronger and deeper over time and through being honest. It means sharing life's joys and the sad times too.

Kristin A. Kunzman

Healthy neutrality is when you care but don't take on the job. . . . This kind of thinking may seem selfish and uncaring. Actually, it's a gift. You give up "fixing" someone and just let them know you love them whether they get "fixed" or not.

Judi Hollis

Life has its ebb and flow, and the assertive person has enough personal security to roll with the punches and adopt a style to fit the occasion. The assertive response to conflict is, "I'm okay and you're okay. If there is a problem between us, we can work it out."

Judi Hollis

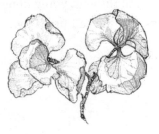

Asking for what you want is a powerful and positive way to develop greater self-confidence, feel better about yourself, and create what you want in your life.

Sheila Bayle-Lissick and Elise Marquam Jahns

*W*hen love is without power, we take care of others at our own emotional expense. When power is without love, we abuse, hurt, and injure others—ultimately at our own expense. Our task, then, is to build affirming relationships—the peak experience of all peak experiences—where love and power are in balance.

Brenda Schaeffer

Our relationships are laboratories for our spiritual growth and awakening.

Molly Young Brown

Fortunately, the greatest benefits of honesty come not from living up to the impossible standard of perfection but from the more modest and sustainable goal of gradual self-improvement.

Lewis M. Andrews

My pride does not need to have the first and last word. I can take the time to think things through and feel my feelings. Then my pride will sit back and allow my true power to emerge.

Maureen Brady

Don't look for sympathy. Remember the old saying "Sympathy kills" and look for people who will understand but who will encourage you to help yourself. You may need understanding and compassion, but you don't need sympathy!

Terence Williams

Philosophers, poets, scientists, and artists have all thought about and written about the human potential. We know the depths of brutality which are possible for humans and also the brilliance and saintliness. To tap into our own potential, however, we need to bring these notions home to ourselves as individuals. We are, each one of us, the stuff that dreams are made of; we each create dreams, and we can and do bring at least some of our dreams into being, for the benefit of the world.

Molly Young Brown

Humans are not perfect creatures and never will be. If we tell ourselves and others we must strive to be perfect, we are setting ourselves and others up for very stressful, frustrating, and painful lives. We will be pushing ourselves and others away from humanity—where our strength and spirit are to be found.

Craig Nakken

By asserting yourself to make amends, you assert your rightful place as an equal member of the human race—no less and no greater than all other people.

Roseann Lloyd and Merle Fossum

Just as we are called to serve others, others are called to serve us. Sometimes it is a greater challenge to accept another's love and assistance than it is to offer our own service.

Molly Young Brown

Everyday frustrations can become our spiritual teachers, reminding us where we cling to our fixed notions of how things should be. Even major crises and personal losses can serve as powerful vehicles with which we can soften and transform our character defects.

Phillip Z.

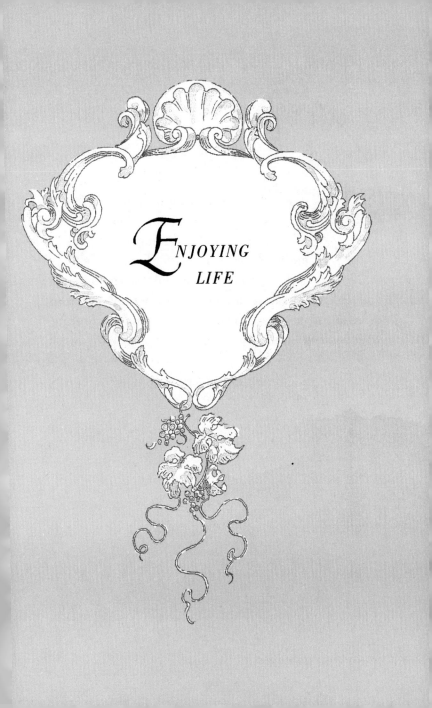

ENJOYING LIFE

hat do I want?" This is probably the hardest question we can ask ourselves. And it's an important question to answer because it determines how we live our lives. Think about it for a while. It's an important enough question to spend the entire day thinking about, dreaming about, reaching deep inside, and discovering what we really want.

Perry Tilleraas

Creative activity immerses us fully in the here and now, and at the same time it frees us. We become one with the activity and are nourished by it. We grow as the activity grows. We learn who we are in the very process of not thinking about who we are.

Karen Casey

When we are living as our unique selves, we find we have a rich creativity available to us. We know how people are when they fall in love. They are a little silly, do unexpected things, and are freer than we are used to seeing them. Creativity is like that. We love into existence that which we wish to create. I believe that what we create also contains the love that brought us into existence.

Ruth Schweitzer-Mordecai

Though perhaps hidden, there is a person inside me who wants to have fun, an inner child who knows the joys of living. Even in dark moments, my inner child may smile and tease and help me see a bit of humor. From these times of brief sunlight, when I laugh out loud and wonder at the sound, I realize my life must include this humor.

Will Limon

Success is to do what you want to do. Failure is to not do it.

Joe Klaas

*M*ost of us yearn for relatively simple things:
to express ourselves creatively, to feel a
common bond with people, to give our love and be loved in
return. We deserve to experience these heartfelt desires.
And we are capable of bringing them into our lives.

Helene Lerner-Robbins

We deserve to treat ourselves well. And we can't really serve others well unless we do.

Helene Lerner-Robbins

All we need is already ours if we believe it to be so. Our challenge is being open to receive it and gracious enough to appreciate it.

Helene Lerner-Robbins

I have in my world, and in myself, all the richness I could ever ask for and more than I will ever fully appreciate. Just having the opportunity to sit here this morning and feel what I am feeling, think what I am thinking, write what I am writing—that's my rightful treasure.

Eliot Alexander

The faith that we are cared for even when we don't quite understand what's going on is a gift. We get ready to receive the gift by giving up our misguided sense of independence and opening ourselves to the care that surrounds us. It does not come from just one person but from many.

Elizabeth L.

I look back and see that the separate pieces of my life have fit together to form a meaningful pattern. One event has led to another. One door has closed so another could open. It makes sense. While the events were happening, I was often anxious and perplexed. Worrying about the future robbed me of peace in the present. In reality, I have no control over whether or not the sun will rise tomorrow, nor can I control what the days, weeks, and years ahead will bring to me. What I can do is learn to trust God's pattern as it unfolds one day at a time.

Elizabeth L.

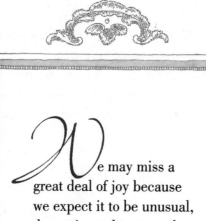

We may miss a great deal of joy because we expect it to be unusual, dramatic, and spectacular. We are waiting for lights to flash and bells to ring. But the truth is that joy is here, right now, waiting for us to notice it.

Veronica Ray

If we don't believe today is the greatest gift we could receive, we'll never know how to live for today. Everything we want to achieve, to learn, to share can begin today. If we don't live the best we can right now, then when?

Amy E. Dean

We can seek help from others. We can return to the sources of hope and strength in our life, and we can keep in contact with them. What's more, we can be grateful. We can treasure the moments of joy, laughter, ease, and contentment with the people we love, knowing that these are ours forever.

Mel Pohl, Deniston Kay, and Doug Toft

We learn to live well the same way we gain skill or any art or craft—from others who serve as our coaches or teachers and by the daily routine of practice, discipline, and hard work.

Merle Fossum

So before you do anything else, just "be."
Be present to your own character. Be with it, without
fighting it. Be in your life, as it is.

Roseann Lloyd and Merle Fossum

Although it might feel wonderful to be the
center of attention for awhile, most of us discover that it
also feels good to care about others. We begin to recognize
that a world of shared attention is also a world of mutual
warmth and comfort. We trade off the need to be the only
person in the universe for our contribution to the safety
and beauty of the community.

Ronald Potter-Efron and Patricia Potter-Efron

My reason for being on earth may be obscure, but my function is not. My function is to be myself, to be loving, to forgive. If I can learn that and impart it to someone else, my mission will be accomplished.

Mark L.

Sometimes it feels like I can't catch my breath between life's lessons, running and straining to keep up. But if I hold tight, buoyed by God's strength, I can fly.

Heidi Waldrop

Are you ready and willing to become a person who actively responds to the good things in life?

Judi Hollis

Mindfulness requires us to look at the essence of the now and to feel the joy of the moment. The joy comes from the process of *doing* an activity rather than *finishing* the activity.

Sheila Bayle-Lissick and Elise Marquam Jahns

Out of its abysses, unpredictable life unfolds, with a never-ending procession of miracles, crises, healing, and growth. Sometimes what happens is painful, tragic, seemingly unbearable to us mortals. Yet somehow life continues, also yielding an ample supply of beauty, pleasure, and fulfillment. When I realize this, once again, I also see the absurdity of my belief that I can understand, predict, and control life. All I can really do is go along for the ride, with as much consciousness and love as I can muster in the moment.

Molly Young Brown

Good friends are treasures. They nurture me with enthusiasm and help me reflect on myself with their honest feedback. They become a constellation around me, a network in which I feel located and oriented.

Maureen Brady

J have been given joy as a gift, and I do not need to deny myself its experience and expression. Instead I can recognize it as a feeling with the potential to heal me.

Maureen Brady

LETTING GO

The truth is, we already possess everything we need. We carry around our source of wholeness wherever we go. Only when we stop the frantic search for something out there do we realize that the path to happiness leads inside. Only when we slow down and take time to breathe and bring our attention back to our inner selves do we find the love we've been looking for.

Perry Tilleraas

If nothing ever went wrong, we wouldn't need serenity. How would we know if we had serenity without troubles to use it on? Success and happiness are not reached by denying we have difficulties. We arrive at success and happiness by surrounding difficulties.

Joe Klaas

*T*oday let me realize I am responsible for much of the discomfort I feel. Since my attitudes have helped create the painful problem, I also have within me the healthy attitudes to solve it. I will work through my pain and heal self-limiting thoughts which prevent me from realizing my wholeness.

Liane Cordes

Real power comes when we stop holding others responsible for our pain, and we take responsibility for all our feelings.

Melody Beattie

 Yet, with each ending comes room for another beginning. Whether we realize it or not, we choose from within what our lives are to be each day, each hour, *each thought.* Beginning again is realizing that choice. Beginning again is grieving and feeling anger through this loss, honoring the relationship, and letting go of it so we may continue to live. Beginning again is seeing the promise in the pain and our growth through this change.

Will Limon

Letting go isn't easy. Especially if we confuse letting go with not caring.

Earnie Larsen and Carol Larsen Hegarty

The experiences that challenge us the most are perhaps our greatest gifts: the job that we were fired from helped launch a new career; a divorce that created many sleepless nights led us to develop our spirituality; the acknowledgment of our weaknesses brought us to greater self-acceptance. Growing through pain refines our character.

Helene Lerner-Robbins

If sadness is the order of the day for today, then so be it. We will learn, and we will grow, and there will be more room in our hearts for laughter tomorrow (or maybe even later today).

Elizabeth L.

I didn't know hurt goes away faster if one is willing to feel it, perhaps shed some tears, and let it pass, instead of spending huge amounts of energy denying it. I'm learning I can say no and watch a relationship deepen instead of disappear. I'm learning I can like myself even though I'm not perfect. I'm learning that letting down my guard and telling it like it is brings others closer rather than pushing them away.

Elizabeth L.

We often hear the phrase "when one door shuts, another opens." It means everything has a beginning and an end. When our travels on one path are completed, another path lies ahead.

Amy E. Dean

It hurts to remove those pieces of glass, but it also gives the foot a chance to heal. On the other side of resentment is love. On the other side of fear is calmness.

Mel Pohl, Deniston Kay, and Doug Toft

All people facing a life crisis are called upon to respond to their problem with something new from within—perhaps from an inner resource they never used before. The same old coping response either doesn't fit the new reality or it might be exactly what led to the current problem.

Merle Fossum

The death of a relationship is painful, but mature people have enough respect for themselves and their partners to cope when love is over. Mature people know how to let go of an unsalvageable relationship, just as they are able to survive crisis in a healthy one. Even in their grief, they do not doubt they will love again someday.

Brenda Schaeffer

You can't change the past, but you can understand it, and you can make friends with it as much as possible.

Kristin A. Kunzman

Life doesn't always work out the way we want. It's important to know when to stop and try a different strategy.

John Hough and Marshall Hardy

The Quakers have a beautiful phrase: "Pray with moving feet." In other words, we need to invest all our effort and energy to make sure that we achieve our goals and dreams. But once we've prayed with moving feet, we do need to let go and trust that what happens will not only be right for us but will happen when the time is right.

Sheila Bayle-Lissick and Elise Marquam Jahns

Today I can sit still with my losses, letting the appropriate sadness reside in my heart until it is ready to pass on and open me to new friends.

Maureen Brady

Among the many things that keep us wrapped up in someone else's problems is our fear—our apprehension. We're usually so worried about what will happen next that we don't see how we are keeping the pot boiling in spite of ourselves. We can't see how our own behavior provides phony reasons for the troubled person's behavior, how our eagerness to save the day or to cover up the problem helps it to go on.

Terence Williams

We do not need to press ourselves about forgiveness, but we do need to be willing to feel that gentle tap our higher power sometimes gives to our shoulder. A whisper that says, "You do not have to carry this weight by holding on to hatred about everything that happened in the past."

Maureen Brady

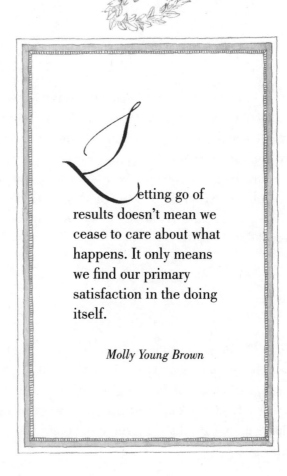

Letting go of results doesn't mean we cease to care about what happens. It only means we find our primary satisfaction in the doing itself.

Molly Young Brown

God grant me serenity
to accept the things I cannot change,
courage to change the things I can,
and wisdom to know the difference.

Reinhold Niebuhr

A U T H O R I N D E X

The following books are all published by Hazelden.

Stephanie Abbott et al., *Talk, Trust and Feel.* © 1991
Eliot Alexander, *Sick and Tired of Being Fat.* © 1990
Lewis M. Andrews, *Happiness and Honesty.* © 1991
Mark L., *Stairway to Serenity.* © 1988
Sheila Bayle-Lissick and Elise Marquam Jahns, *Creating Choices.*
    © 1990
Melody Beattie, *Beyond Codependency.* © 1989
———. *Codependent No More.* © 1987
———. *The Language of Letting Go.* © 1990
Maureen Brady, *Daybreak.* © 1991
Molly Young Brown, *Growing Whole.* © 1993
Karen Casey, *Each Day a New Beginning.* © 1982
Jean Illsley Clarke and Connie Dawson, *Growing Up Again.* © 1989
Liane Cordes, *The Reflecting Pond.* © 1981
Amy E. Dean, *Night Light.* © 1986
Merle Fossum, *Catching Fire.* © 1989
Judi Hollis, *Fat Is a Family Affair.* © 1985
John Hough and Marshall Hardy, *Against the Wall.* © 1991
Joe Klaas, *The Twelve Steps to Happiness.* © 1982
Kristin A. Kunzman, *The Healing Way.* © 1990
Elizabeth L., *Food for Thought.* © 1980
———. *Listen to the Hunger.* © 1987
Earnie Larsen and Carol Larsen Hegarty, *Days of Healing, Days of Joy.*
    © 1987
Helene Lerner-Robbins, *Embrace Change.* © 1992
———. *My Timing Is Always Right.* © 1992
Will Limon, *Beginning Again.* © 1991
Marie Lindquist, *Holding Back.* © 1987
Roseann Lloyd and Merle Fossum, *True Selves.* © 1991
Craig Nakken, *The Addictive Personality.* © 1988
Mel Pohl, Deniston Kay, and Doug Toft, *The Caregivers' Journey.*
    © 1990
Ronald Potter-Efron and Patricia Potter-Efron, *Letting Go of Shame.*
    © 1989

Veronica Ray, *Accepting Ourselves.* © 1989
———. *Choosing Happiness.* © 1991
———. *Letting Go.* © 1989
———. *Living Our Own Lives.* © 1989
———. *Setting Boundaries.* © 1989
Gayle Rosellini and Mark Worden, *Of Course You're Angry.* © 1985
Brenda Schaeffer, *Is It Love or Is It Addiction?* © 1987
———. *Loving Me, Loving You.* © 1991
Ruth Schweitzer-Mordecai, *Spiritual Freedom.* © 1991
Perry Tilleraas, *The Color of Light.* © 1988
Heidi Waldrop, *Showing Up for Life.* © 1990
———.et al., *Womanspirit.* © 1992
Terence Williams, *Do's and Dont's.* © 1982
Phillip Z., *A Skeptic's Guide to the Twelve Steps.* © 1990

INDEX OF FIRST LINES